Lionheart Summer

Kevin Densley

Lionheart Summer

PICARO PRESS

to my family

Lionheart Summer
ISBN 978 1 921691 20 1
Copyright © text Kevin Densley 2011
Cover: an illustration of Richard I Cour de Lion from a 12th century codex, licenced under http://creativecommons.org/licenses/by-sa/3.0/, available at http://commons.wikimedia.org/wiki/File:Richard_coeurdelion_g.jpg

First published by Picaro Press 2011

This edition published 2018 by
Picaro Press – an imprint of
GINNINDERRA PRESS
PO Box 3461 Port Adelaide 5015 Australia
www.ginninderrapress.com.au

Contents

Lionheart Summer	7
The Anni-Frid, Björn, Benny and Agnetha Syndrome	9
Ben Hall's Photograph	10
In the Good Old Days	11
Morning Sun, Fitzroy	12
To Dionysus	13
The Erotic Wisdom of the East	14
Image Suggested by a Cinema Usher	15
with Whom I Used to Work,	15
an Aspiring Conceptual Artist,	15
Whose Name I Can't Remember	15
Brother and Sister	16
A Response to Geoff Page's 'On the Death of a Famous Cricketer'	17
At Campbell's Creek Cemetery, Victoria	18
I Hear Motion	24
Stone and Darkness	25
After Reading Kenneth Tynan's Review of John Osborne's *Luther*	27
Morrisons, Victoria	28
Prince Albert Hotel, Daylesford, Victoria	29
Morning in My Backyard	30
Picture Perfect	31
Archetypal Dream	32
Another for Mr Malley	33
Amherst Wisdom	34
Drifting into Oblivion	35
Every Odyssey	36
Limeburners' Point, Geelong	37
Fun-o-Rama	38
The Artist Formerly Known	39

Holiday	40
Dealey Plaza, November 22	41
The New Testament	43
Oedipus and the Theban Sphinx	45
George Stubbs's *A Lion Attacking a Horse*	46
Larger than Life	47
Mum's Map of Tassie	48
Vigil	49
surreal redwheelbarrow	50
To Janus, God of Doorways	51
Little Generalissimos	52
Postmodernism	53
'Poets never die'	54
My Raven	55
Acknowledgements	56

Lionheart Summer

Adelaide, 1980

The vines twisted around the pergola
in my grandmother's backyard
were gnarled and old;
the afternoon heat unbearable.
But when evening came
the sea breeze wafted through
and we'd sit outside drinking beer or wine
until darkness fell.
Inside the bluestone house,
the temperature never rose;
afternoons I'd fold
into a comfy chair,
frosty Southwark Bitter in hand,
and watch test cricket on TV.
Or else I'd lounge in the parlour,
on the carpet, near the piano,
leafing through sheet music like 'Ramona',
a South Seas maiden on its sepia title page.
On the wall was a hand-tinted photo
of my step-grandfather in soldier garb,
blue-eyed and full of vigour,
taken before New Guinea.
Now he'd be coughing
in the next room, battling
emphysema and losing.
That summer at my grandmother's,
I'd bought Kate Bush's *Lionheart* LP.
Flame-haired English beauty Kate

posed on the cover in a lionsuit,
a pantomime lion head nearby.
A song on her record
was the summer's refrain:
Oh England, my lionheart,
I'm in your garden
fading fast in your arms…

The Anni-Frid, Björn, Benny and Agnetha Syndrome

Every Scandinavian,
at some point in their lives,
has a perfect body
and their seventies pop stars
live in sixteenth-century castles
in the Alps where Byron and Shelley raved,
summer at St Tropez, Portofino,
with faded European royalty,
retired Ferrari executives,
bronzed embezzlers in sailing suits
and topless-sunbathing pendulous-breasted
middle-aged Italian
fashion house heiresses,
breed racehorses, become
art experts, wine connoisseurs,
and look more elegant now
than at the height of their fame.

Ben Hall's Photograph

Though to many Ben Hall is an oft-reproduced
daguerreotype of a handsome man,
taken in a Sydney studio
in the late eighteen-fifties,
one of those old, faded civil war types
of photographs which blanch the face,
highlight the black/white contrasts
and make the sitter seem
forlorn, romantic and doomed
– and photographs so often lie –
in Ben's sad case,
his picture
pretty much did him justice.

In the Good Old Days

mass murderers had crew cuts,
wore horn-rimmed glasses,
were Protestant Caucasian males
and lived in middle America.
They bought their polyester shirts from K-Mart,
had pencils and pens in their front pockets
for no apparent reason
and, when finally captured,
after committing their awful crimes,
were photographed against whitewashed walls
of sleepy small-town cop stations,
vague, forlorn expressions
upon their unshaven faces.
When interviewed on the six o'clock news,
their neighbours always remarked
how 'quiet' they were,
'real gentlemen',
'good with children' too.
These county townsfolk would gaze
from the footpaths of peaceful, tree-lined streets
at the house of the perpetrator
which, we were disturbed to see,
looked very much like our own.

Morning Sun, Fitzroy

Morning sun
on Smith Street
light and beautiful.

Beer and wine bottles
littering the footpaths
glint with rainbows.

To Dionysus

Transvestite god,
your dress is very pretty
but it does not suit:
you are too big and bulky.
And your make up,
while applied with care,
looks silly – that plum lipstick shrieks
'I am such a dickhead!'
As for the laurel wreath
adorning your flaxen hair…
what the hell is that about?
Stop slurping wine from golden goblets
and running madly through fields
pursued by crazy women.
Desist from hallucinogenics,
wild parties and kinky sex!
And if I see another lyre
thrown from an inn window…
You're not as young as you once were.
I'm serious, mate. It's embarrassing.

The Erotic Wisdom of the East

Why does the Kama Sutra
use the term 'sexual congress'?
It sounds like a senate sitting
where everyone's randy.

Image Suggested by a Cinema Usher with Whom I Used to Work, an Aspiring Conceptual Artist, Whose Name I Can't Remember

A pair of jeans
propped up in a corner
filled with cauliflowers.

Brother and Sister

i.m. Thomas Scrimgeour and his sister Elizabeth, my great-grandmother

There's the studio portrait
of Thomas, a great-great-uncle,
in Australian Imperial Forces garb,
hands behind back, upright,
gazing at the camera lens.
He poses in front of a backdrop
depicting a camp of army tents
under wispy, optimistic skies.

Six months later Thomas died of wounds
as a German POW,
shot through the lungs,
lost in the maelstrom of Fromelles.
Fritz, a great bookkeeper,
recorded his death for posterity.

*

I never met Elizabeth,
his sister.
She died in a distant country town
when I was eight.
The only memory I possess
is my family waiting outside her house
– I must have been about five.
Someone eventually knocked on the door,
but there was nobody home.

A Response to Geoff Page's 'On the Death of a Famous Cricketer'

A biased bloke, a quiet bigot,
he possessed the common sense
not to parade his lesser side
before an adoring public.

He was part of a Mason/Catholic divide
in his test side during the thirties,
'liked to hear the sound of his own voice'
according to Len Hutton.

Was blunt as a sawn-off twenty-two
when the cricket wasn't up to scratch.
'Geez, you bowled some rubbish, son,'
he once chided a young Test bowler.

A man who seemed to dislike
the public's unstinting gaze,
yet couldn't have done without it:
it made him who he was.

Cocky and smug, this little chap,
antithesis of the Aussie 'mate',
with the sporting genius's age-old curse
of not fitting in with the team.

At Campbell's Creek Cemetery, Victoria

Campbell's Creek Cemetery,
five miles from Castlemaine,
starts off as flat land
then snakes up a rocky, Golgothan hill.
Many of its earliest graves,
dating from 1852,
are no longer marked.
Some older headstones lie,
broken off at the base,
against an embankment on one side,
flecked with lichen,
inscriptions worn by wind and rain,
blanched by sun.
On a hot February morning,
I travelled there,
hoping to find the grave
of my great-great-great-grandfather
who died on the Castlemaine goldfields
of dysentery, in 1852.
He'd joined the throng from Van Diemen's Land,
with a son, to try his luck.
I approached the caretaker's office.
He wandered out,
a short, stocky man
in T-shirt, shorts and work boots.
Not very hospitable.
I probably looked like a tourist
which, in part, I was.
But his attitude annoyed me.
I had another, better reason
for being there.

Somewhere in this cemetery
my ancestor's mortal remains
lay buried.
I wondered what they looked like now.
A skull and bones, brown with age?
Scraps of dried out skin? Tufts of hair?
I told the caretaker why I had come.
'Go and have a look,' he said.
'Most of the older graves are up there.'
He gestured towards the hill.
'Thanks,' I said, without meaning it,
heading in that direction.
'Beware of tigers,' he yelled,
probably smirking at the thought
of putting the wind up a tourist.
Tiger snakes didn't worry me, though.
I'd seen some as a kid.
'A snake will only attack
if sick or cornered,'
someone told me back then.
I wandered through the graves,
reading names and dates.
A cemetery's always full of stories,
but I didn't find part of mine.
Returning to the caretaker's office,
I muttered to myself,
'Great bloody help he was.'
As I entered, the rough-headed bloke
was poring over a ledger,
enormous, old and leather-bound.

He looked up. An odd vignette,
this bushy reading a giant book.
'What was your relative's name again?'
'Densley,' I answered.
'When did he die?'
'January, 1852.'
He flicked back some pages,
then placed his finger decisively.
'There,' he said, turning the book towards me.
To my surprise, he'd found the record
of my great-great-great-grandfather's burial,
written in a stylish, old-fashioned hand.
'Densley, Thomas,' he continued.
'He was the seventy-third person buried here,
in the C of E section.
It says, "Occupation: stonemason." '
This fact seemed to interest him.
'You know, he probably helped build
some of our early bridges and pubs.
Each stonemason had his own special mark
and if you knew what that was, you could –'
'I knew he was a stonemason,' I cut in,
impatient for more information
as to where he had been buried.
'He learnt the trade as a convict.
Around here, though,
I think he was mainly a prospector.'
'Fair enough,' said the caretaker,
pulling out a plan
for the 'Proposed Campbell's Creek Cemetery, 1851'.

(I was surprised it still existed
– it's amazing what survives
in the archives of country towns.)
'Where his grave would probably be,' he said,
'is over there.'

He pointed out the door.
'Though most of that section's been buried over.'
'Thanks. Thanks a lot,' I nodded,
wanting to leave the shed.
I'd noticed there were still a few
old graves among the newer ones
in the C of E section.
I might be in luck.
The bloke became loquacious.
'Every so often, the older graves
get buried over,' he went on.
'To save on space.
And sometimes in a family plot,
if the children all died young,
they'd put their coffins one on top of the other.'
'Interesting,' I said, departing,
keen to continue my search.
I looked among the C of E graves.
Most were recent – 1950s onwards.
It was easy to tell these newest plots
– no angels reaching for heaven,
prayerful Virgins or Latin adorned them.
They had plain white stones with names and dates.

Among the old ones,
I couldn't find my ancestor's.
I wondered when his headstone disappeared.
Who was at his funeral? Did he even have one?
Had his grave been tended, ever,
by people who cared?
But before I left the cemetery,
I was struck by a family plot,
over a century old.
Mother, father and their six children
were all entombed.
What made me pause
was the children.

None lived to adulthood.
A son reached his teens,
a daughter, twelve;
the rest died before five.
Mother and father outlived them all.
I drove away from the cemetery,
thinking of the parents' grief.
How did they cope,
burying all six children?
Even back then, in less healthy times,
usually a couple
survived to maturity.
My great-great-great-grandfather
died in his early fifties,
but at least he'd had a vivid life
and children who'd borne children.

Indeed, the strongest memory
of my visit to Campbell's Creek
is those poor parents and their six children.
My endeavour to find a nugget
of family history
had been to no avail.
Looking back, it is no surprise:
I'd been digging, like my ancestor,
in unyielding earth.

I Hear Motion

At the outskirts of Ocean Grove,
headlights on gravel roads
penetrate the darkness.
Sand dunes, rambling salt-bush.
In a car with my first lover,
our relationship fraught, almost over.
Song on the radio.
For a moment, we're not doomed.
'I Hear Motion' by Models,
my girlfriend's favourite band:
Now let it out, shout to the night
And so it goes, I hear motion
Just count it out, shout in your sleep
You say the word, I hear motion…

At the outskirts of Ocean Grove,
headlights on gravel roads
penetrate the darkness.

Stone and Darkness

before the lighting of the Paschal candle,
Easter Sunday, St Paul's Cathedral, Melbourne

At the side entrance
of the cathedral,
in the biting cold,
we draw our jackets closer.
It's five-thirty in the morning,
the city very quiet,
sky like deep blue velvet,
streaks of yellow light
yet to appear.
The stately procession
from the manse begins
– bishop, deacons,
precentor and priests,
altar boys.
We could be witnessing a scene
of a thousand years ago
in a medieval courtyard
or, perhaps,
from El Greco's Spain…
but there is no miracle conflation
of Earth and Heaven;

no nobleman who did great good
is lowered into his grave
by saints descended from Paradise
dressed in golden vestments;
we do not see the soul ascending
assisted by an angel;
there is no Virgin, miscellaneous
saints and angels,
putti,
what you will,
watching as the soul soars by;
Christ cannot be seen
presiding over all
on His seat of judgement.

And there is no solemn
ruby-lipped boy
dressed in funereal black
standing in the foreground,
pointing to what is going on.

After Reading Kenneth Tynan's Review of John Osborne's *Luther*

Luther and his anus…

Eminent American psychologist,
Erik Eriksen, wrote
that the monk's key moments
were connected to his bowels,
noting his famous 'revelation in the tower'
in fact took place in the privy
and that he was 'plagued by constipation'
throughout his life.

Theatre critic, Ken Tynan,
in a review of Osborne's play, Luther,
referred to Eriksen's study,
further observing that the monk
once commissioned a woodcut
in which Rome was depicted
as a harlot giving rectal birth
to a bevy of misshapen demons.

Osborne's play itself,
according to Mr Tynan,
was inspired by this anality,
revelled in excremental earthiness
and throbbed with a rhetorical zeal
unheard on the English stage
since the seventeenth century.

Morrisons, Victoria

Not a town:
a locality
on a bush road off the highway.
A dry, stony river bed
runs beside the road.
The hill overlooking the absent river
is pocked with old mineshafts.
A farm kid, exploring,
his father at the Great War,
fell in one and was buried alive.
Near the bridge is a small,
immaculately maintained
Mechanics' Institute hall.
But where are the people who'd use it?
Dad told me Uncle Cecil
lived here once.
But that was decades ago.

Prince Albert Hotel, Daylesford, Victoria

Night approaches.
Mist descends
on this mid-winter country town.
The ducks on the lake
huddle close to shore.
In the hills, the honey stall has shut.
Alone, I stand in a back street,
looking at the ruin
of an old stone pub.
I can just make out its name
on a crumbling side wall:
'Prince Albert'. Victoria's beloved.
Was it a pub where families would gather?
Or rough-heads brawl on Saturday nights?
Popular? Poorly patronized?
A few old locals might know.
Judging by what buildings remain,
this town of a mere few thousand
used to have a pub and church
in every second street.
Sin in one, be forgiven in the other:
everything in balance.

Morning in My Backyard

Fat bees bumble
over the sweet
half-eaten meat
in pet food bowls.
Duck-arsed pigeons
strut, chests out.
Cats snooze on the grass
in shade.
Neighbours' dogs bark, randomly,
at canine irritations.

Me drinking coffee,
smoking,
in a deckchair, reading,
fearful of the day ahead.

Picture Perfect

'That's what I like in a woman,' said the truckie,
writing into a men's magazine
about a photo of a totally nude
'Home Girl' in the last edition.
'Natural tits and a thick pubic bush.'

A little reductive, don't you think?

Archetypal Dream

You wander into a forest etc.
The trees are straight and tall etc.
A large black bear appears etc.
You are pursued etc.
The woods become thicker etc.
You arrive at a clearing etc.
The bear seizes you etc.
You fear for your life etc.
But you are surprised etc.
You both start to dance etc.
Let's twist again
like we did last summer
etc.

Another for Mr Malley

Snakes like slippery fingers
remind me of your thoughts.

Rusted white wrought-iron gates
promise indifferent heaven.

Rowdy and impatient,
I caw among the cockatiels.

Listless birds-of-paradise
shower your garden with brilliance.

Amherst Wisdom

Never quote the poem,
'Heart! We will forget him!'
to a lover,
in order to make them realise
how much they've been missing you.

Too often they will think of someone else.

Drifting into Oblivion

In flowing robes of gold, maroon,
purple and lapis lazuli,
a line of women wanders through
this Piero della Francescan room,
their pre-Raphaelite faces impassive, pale
and gazing directly ahead.
Now they have drifted onto divans.
Their Giottoesque poses of lamentation
make the scene so painterly
that I hardly notice them
wilt and expire.

Every Odyssey

At some point,
in every odyssey,
grave self-doubt sets in

– you want to give up,
kill yourself
or crawl into oblivion

forgetting to remember
that everything you've done
has got you this far.

Limeburners' Point, Geelong

You look out from the boat ramp and see,
well, not very much at all
– an aluminium refinery
across a flat lagoon
and, to your left, the drab blue-grey
of Corio Bay.

Disappointing that a place
with such an evocative name
is so bloody boring.

Fun-o-Rama

The Fun-o-Rama,
a corrugated
iron shed near a pub,
had a rough, hand-painted sign
signalling its entrance.
Old pinball machines
lined each side wall.
At the far end was a booth
which framed the sullen bulldog head
of the owner.
As kids, this was a place to avoid:
local gangs held sway.
One humid, rain-spattered night,
just before closing time,
a ferret-faced teenage boy
(his police identikit stared
from the front page of next day's paper) entered.
No other patrons were there.
He stabbed the sullen man to death
with a screwdriver,
then wandered into a life unknown.

The Artist Formerly Known

Pop star Anthony Bonicello,
at the start, was matchstick-thin
and known as Elastic Anthony
because of his supple gymnastic act.
He had a number one hit
with the novelty song 'Bend Me Baby'.
Making use of parallel bars, vaulting horse
and Roman rings, he'd sing
Bend me baby, I'm your plasticine...
But his follow-up single, 'Pliable Me',
sunk like a bathysphere.
What to do next, after Teen Angel records
shanghaied him into the street?
He slicked down his hair,
grew a porn star moustache,
crooning bad cabaret
in front of an ensemble
of overweight, alcoholic,
paid-by-the-hour musicians.
That didn't last long. Poor Anthony
ended up weighing three hundred pounds,
dying, arteries hard as cement,
in the arms of a male whore.
Not that there's anything wrong about that:
they were in love.
But it was sad.

Holiday

We're on the veranda
of a holiday cottage
in the middle of sunlit
native bush.
Below us, bees hover
around lavender,
their buzzing a sweet, warm
musical haze.
We're drinking lush, buttery
chardonnay,
sampling an antipasto platter
entirely of local produce.
Last night, we made love.
Tonight
after a gourmet meal
concluding with chocolates
and black Spanish sherry,
again we'll be naked, spent,
dreamy.

This will never last.

Dealey Plaza, November 22

He's in the zone,
high up there,
on the sixth floor
of the book depository building.
Typical left-wing loony, he'd
sojourned in Soviet Russia,
distributed propaganda leaflets
(an ersatz sixties *Big Issue* seller),
been kicked out of the marines.
Now here he is,
with the rifle,
eye straining through the sight.
The presidential cars approach…
Kennedy's skull explodes.
Governor Connally is shot
through the chest, wrist and thigh.
Who knows how many shots are fired (he doesn't),
especially with his mate on the grassy knoll.
The First Lady climbs
out of the back seat
of the presidential limousine,
covered in her husband's blood.
Oswald throws the rifle aside.

Hurries downstairs,
through bland suburban streets,
shoots a local cop
(this wasn't part of the plan),
is arrested in a picture theatre
where he's smacked about and subdued.
Bombarded with questions by the police.
Day becomes night becomes day.
Then another nutter,
redneck crim, Jack Ruby,
enters from stage-right with a pistol,
mortally wounds him in the guts.
Not long before, Lee Harvey cried out
as he passed the TV cameras,
'I am just a patsy.'
Who knows what he meant.

The New Testament

1. Before the Resurrection

The stone buildings in this land,
blocky and Middle Eastern,
are like a painted backdrop.
Roads flat and grey,
and scenes seem airless, dulled:
horses, camels, asses,
dark-skinned people in desert clothes.
What overrides is a sense
of sparseness,
spaciousness,
as if viewing
events on a stage with minimal props.
Matthew, Mark, Luke and John
must have thought the stories
of this time and place
too important to be cluttered
with quotidian detail.
You distinctly feel
the colourlessness
and want of the decorative.

2. The Resurrection and After

Suddenly the New Testament landscape
is bright and airy.
The marvellous and strange occur
like a magical realist novel.
Some speak in tongues,
Mary is assumed into heaven.
People – Jesus, Lazarus –
rise from the dead.
With surprisingly little fanfare,
Christ disappears
from the world.
Pentecost Sunday,
the Holy Ghost
appears above the Apostles' heads
in vivid tongues of flame.
Christianity is ready to roll,
its theatre the known world.

Oedipus and the Theban Sphinx

Young Oedipus was a clever lad.
He solved the riddle of the Sphinx
who, in despair at what he'd done,
threw herself off a nearby cliff.

An overreaction, surely.

George Stubbs's *A Lion Attacking a Horse*

Poetic lines
of muscle and movement
– the lion sinking his teeth
into the horse's neck,
his razor claws
tearing into its flanks and rump.
Moody, dynamic,
archetypally Romantic:
a lion (Passion) attacking a horse (Reason).
We know which will prevail.
Blake indicated that:
'The tigers of wrath are wiser
than the horses of instruction.'

Larger than Life

The Great Poet, a big man,
in computer-image style,
is morphing into something huge.
Bald head like a billiard ball
disappearing into beanbag body.
Seems he's having a hearty chuckle
at becoming his own weighty world.

Mum's Map of Tassie

seen by all the family,
in bathroom,
bedroom,
fleetingly, down the hallway

before the start of everything,
before the beginning of the world.

Vigil

Ted is in the other room,
dying.
His daughters – one of them, my wife –
are by his bedside,
have been for countless hours.
It could have happened any time
in the last week,
or so they thought.

I've been there with them, too,
much of the time.
And now it seems
extremely close.

The daughters told me, 'Take a break.
It could still be hours.'
So I'm in the hospital canteen,
deserted at 4 a.m.,
watching *King Solomon's Mines*
on a TV bolted to the wall.

The hospital overnight:
white walls, long corridors, silence.
Hardly a nurse to be seen.

The matron tells us to go home,
get some sleep,
at six a.m.
There is nothing more we can do.
She'll raise his dose of morphine.

Dying can take so long.

surreal redwheelbarrow

sometimes the –
redwheelbarrow –
is full of –
sheep's eyes –
and the embryos –
of koalas –
the buggers look –
a little like prawns –
and I want to fill my mouth
with them –

To Janus, God of Doorways

I enter – you're grinning.
I leave – you look tragic.

Two-faced bastard.

Little Generalissimos

'Military strongmen',
the world over,
are under five foot three,
have bad skin
and masturbate frequently.

Postmodernism

is an expression
of the neurotic nature
of contemporary Western culture,
on its way to being a basket case
if it doesn't have therapy soon.

'Poets never die'

Poets never die,
they simply
write-of-passage.

My Raven

In the middle of a nightmare,
during a troubled time,
a raven settled on my arm:
enormous, majestic,
black sheen violet-shot.
With a gentle squeeze of his giant claws,
he cawed into my ear.
For weeks, I didn't comprehend
his other-worldly message
until, one day,
it dawned on me:

'Survive.'

Acknowledgements

Poems in this collection have previously appeared, sometimes in different form, in the following publications: *Blue Dog: Australian Poetry*, *Buzzwords* (UK), *Centoria*, *core*, *Geelong Times*, *The Journal* (UK), *LiNQ*, *micropress oz*, *Monkey Kettle* (UK), *Orbis* (UK), *Other Poetry* (UK), *Platform*, *Polestar*, *Quadrant*, *Tamba* and *Vernacular*. Thanks to the editors of these publications.

A special nod of appreciation, also, to those friends who have helped me in the shaping of this collection.

Song lyric snippets have been used in the following poems: 'Lionheart Summer', 'I Hear Motion' and 'Archetypal Dream'. The songs concerned, respectively, are 'Oh England, My Lionheart' (by Kate Bush, featured on her *Lionheart* album, EMI, 1978), 'I Hear Motion' (by Models, featured on their *The Pleasure of Your Company* album, Mushroom, 1983) and 'Let's Twist Again' (by Kal Mann and Dave Appell, featured on a single by Chubby Checker, Parkway Records, 1961). The song lyric snippet in 'The Artist Formerly Known' is fictitious.

www.ingramcontent.com/pod-product-compliance
Lightning Source LLC
Chambersburg PA
CBHW071037080526
44587CB00015B/2651